Around the World

Transport

Margaret Hall

Heinemann
LIBRARY

www.heinemann/library.co.uk
Visit our website to find out more information about Heinemann Library books.

To order:
 Phone 44 (0) 1865 888066
 Send a fax to 44 (0) 1865 314091
 Visit the Heinemann Library Bookshop at www.heinemann/library.co.uk to browse our catalogue and order online.

First published in Great Britain by Heinemann Library, Halley Court, Jordan Hill, Oxford OX2 8EJ, a division of Reed Educational and Professional Publishing Ltd. Heinemann is a registered trademark of Reed Educational and Professional Publishing Ltd.

OXFORD MELBOURNE AUCKLAND JOHANNESBURG BLANTYRE
GABORONE IBADAN PORTSMOUTH (NH) USA CHICAGO

Designed by Lisa Buckley
Originated by Dot Gradations
Printed in Hong Kong/China

ISBN 0 431 15123 7 (hardback)
06 05 04 03 02
10 9 8 7 6 5 4 3 2 1

British Library Cataloguing in Publication Data
Hall, Margaret
Transport. - (Around the world)
1.Transportation - Juvenile literature
I.Title
388

Acknowledgements
The publishers would like to thank the following for permission to reproduce photographs: Oliver Benn/Tony Stone, pp. 1, 20; Wolfgang Kaehler, pp., 4a; Keren Su/Tony Stone, p. 4b; Sharon Smith/Bruce Coleman, Inc., p. 4c; Tony Freeman/Photo Edit, pp., 5, 13; Glen Allison/Tony Stone, p. 6; Robert Van Der Hilst/Tony Stone, p. 7; Art Wolfe/Tony Stone, p. 8; David Young-Wolff/Photo Edit, p. 9; Keith Wood/Tony Stone, p.10; J.C. Carton/Bruce Coleman, Inc., p. 11; D. MacDonald/Photo Edit, p. 12; Rudi Von Briel/Photo Edit, p. 14; Bill Bachmann/Photo Edit, pp. 15, 19; Joe McDonald/Bruce Coleman, Inc., p. 16; F. Greenberg/Photo Edit, p. 17; Paul Conklin/Photo Edit, p. 18; Bob Stovall/Bruce Coleman, Inc., p. 21; Robert Brenner/Photo Edit, p. 22; Kent Foster/Bruce Coleman, Inc., p. 23; Kenneth Jarecke/The Stock Market, p. 24; Anna E. Zuckermann/Photo Edit, p. 25; David Madison/Bruce Coleman, Inc., p. 26; Kim Saar/Heinemann Library, p. 27; Andy Sacks/Tony Stone, p. 28; R. Rainey/Photo Edit, p. 29.

Cover photograph reproduced with permission of Robert Van Der Hilst/Tony Stone.

Every effort has been made to contact copyright holders of any material reproduced in this book. Any omissions will be rectified in subsequent printings if notice is given to the publishers.

Any words appearing in the text in bold, **like this**, are explained in the glossary.

Contents

People have needs

People everywhere have the same **needs**.
They need food, clothing, water and
homes. They also need to be able to get
from place to place.

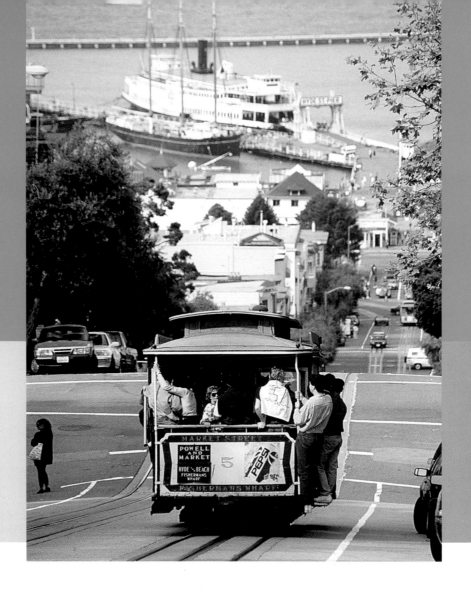

Where people live makes a difference to what they eat and wear. It makes a difference to their homes and the kinds of **transport** they use.

Why people travel

People travel for many reasons. They go to work and school. They go to places to buy or gather things they need.

People also travel for fun. They visit family and friends who live in other cities or countries. Some people travel to see new places or to go on holiday.

Transport around the world

Transport is what moves people or **goods** from place to place. In different places around the world, there are different kinds of transport.

Some kinds of transport can move large numbers of people. Others carry only a few people at a time.

Transporting goods

Many people use **goods** that come from
other places. These goods must be moved
from where they are made or grown.

How goods are moved depends on what they are. It also depends on their **value** and how far they have to travel.

Transport long ago and today

Transport is always changing. Long ago, people walked or rode on animals. They still do. Today, though, people also travel in faster ways.

Inventions in transport have made travel easier and faster. Riding a bicycle is faster than walking. Travelling by car or another **motor vehicle** is even faster.

Travel using feet

Walking is the oldest way of getting about. Most people travel **on foot** sometimes. Even people who own cars often walk, unless they have far to go.

In some places, people use their feet to move **passengers**. They run pulling little carts, or they pedal bicycles that have small cabs attached.

Travel using animals

In many places, animals are used for **transport**. People ride horses, oxen, camels and even elephants. Sometimes the animals pull carts or wagons with **passengers** inside.

Pack animals are used to move **goods** from place to place. The animals carry parcels, bundles and even large boxes on their backs.

Travel by water

In some places, there are not many roads, or the roads are very crowded. It may be easier for people there to travel on rivers, lakes and **canals**.

Many kinds of boats are used to move people, cars and other **goods**. Some boats go short distances. Others can travel all the way across an ocean.

Travel by road

Some kinds of **transport** need roads.
Many roads are not much more than
dirt or **gravel** paths. Others are wide and
smooth so that it is easy to travel quickly.

Bicycles, cars, buses and trucks travel
on roads. In some places there are miles
and miles of good roads. People there
often travel by **motor vehicle**.

Travel by rail

Trains and **trams** move along on **rails** or tracks. Rail travel is important in large cities. People can travel faster by underground train than they can on crowded streets.

Trains are very important in places where there are few good roads. Some rail **systems** cover short distances. Others go across many different countries.

Travel by air

Planes are used to travel long distances quickly. Some planes carry hundreds of people. Some planes are smaller and carry only a few people.

Sometimes the only way to get somewhere is by plane. In places where there are not many roads, small planes can land in a field. A seaplane can even land on water.

Moving large groups of people

In large cities, many people travel at the same time. Special kinds of **transport** are used, such as buses, and underground and **commuter** trains.

In most cities, many people travel in **motor vehicles**. People do not always use cars and buses, though. Some cities have commuter boats!

In the future

Transport scientists and **inventors** work to find better ways to travel. They think about ways to make transport that is faster, safer and easier to use.

Soon, more people might drive electric cars. Trains might move at even higher speeds. Whatever happens, all over the world people will still be moving from place to place.

Photo list

Glossary

canal waterway that people have made

commuter person travelling between home and work

goods things that will be sold to people

gravel small stones

invention useful object that no one has thought of before

inventor someone who thinks of new ideas and objects

motor vehicle any form of transport that uses a motor

needs things people must have in order to live

on foot by walking

pack animal animal, such as a donkey or camel, that is used to carry things

passenger traveller who rides or is carried to where he or she is going

rail track on which vehicles travel

system group of things that work together

tram bus-like vehicle that travels on tracks set into a street

transport ways to move people and goods from place to place

value how much something is worth

More books to read

Bicycles by Chris Oxlade, Heinemann Library, 2000

Boats and Ships by Chris Oxlade, Heinemann Library, 2000

Cars by Chris Oxlade, Heinemann Library, 2000

On the Move by Henry Pluckrose, Franklin Watts, 1998

Planes by Chris Oxlade, Heinemann Library, 2000

Take Care on the Road by Carole Wale, Hodder Wayland, 1998

Index

Titles in the *Around the World* series include:

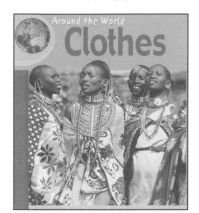

| Hardback | 0 431 15120 2 |

| Hardback | 0 431 15130 X |

| Hardback | 0 431 15121 0 |

| Hardback | 0 431 15131 8 |

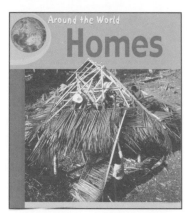

| Hardback | 0 431 15122 9 |

| Hardback | 0 431 15132 6 |

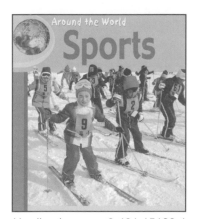

| Hardback | 0 431 15133 4 |

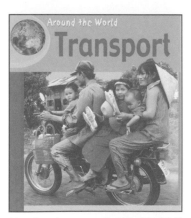

| Hardback | 0 431 15123 7 |

Find out about the other titles in this series on our website www.heinemann.co.uk/library